THOMAS CLARK of Ca

The Village Choir, by Thomas Webster, 1847. (See page 53).
(Thomas Clark is depicted playing the clarionet and John Francis, senior, conducting).

Thomas Clark
of Canterbury
(1775-1859)

by Wallace Harvey

First printed January 1983

© WALLACE HARVEY

All rights reserved. No part of this book
may be reproduced in any way without
permission from the publishers.

ISBN 0 9508564 0 1

Text set in Baskerville 11pt

*Printed and Published in Great Britain by
Emprint, 9 Harbour Street, Whitstable, Kent CT5 1AG*

THOMAS CLARK OF CANTERBURY

In every age and generation our ancient cities and towns have made their own particular impression on the sands of time by the quality of the sons they have produced.

Canterbury in Kent, overshadowed by its glorious cathedral, has throughout the centuries made a rich contribution to the worship of the Christian church by the religious music which its sons have been inspired to compose.

According to the needs of the church and the taste prevailing at the particular time local musicians have been found willing to dedicate their talents to the glory of God, and the result of their labours has enriched the worship of all denominations throughout the world.

As has been the case with all great religious revivals, the impact of the great Methodist revival found its ready response in the metropolitan city. Until that time, in fact ever since the Reformation, the English church had expressed its most joyous tones in the heavy doleful strains of the old German chorales associated with the Sternhold and Hopkins version of the Psalms.

Then came the great spiritual revival which changed the whole outlook of the church. Initiated by Isaac Watts and continued by Charles Wesley the practice of hymn singing swept through the country with invigorating freshness. The ordinary people learned to sing with a vigour never known before. The continous flow of inspiring hymns from the pens of those who were spiritually moved created the need for tunes to which they could be sung.

Musicians in all walks of life were found able to supply that need and the revival was borne on wings of song. During a period of some seventy years, say from 1780 to 1850 many men from the humble walks of life found an unexpected talent for composing singable hymn tunes, and gained enough popular support to have their tunes published. The somewhat florid tunes of that period, while fashionably decryed by an age which considered itself to be more refined, continued to find popular favour and many have found a welcome place in our modern tune books. While it must be admitted that the popular runs and interchange between the parts of those tunes would make many of them too difficult for the capacity of modern congregations, yet nevertheless many are still sung with much appreciation.

Canterbury has produced a number of humble composers of those old hymn tunes eminently worthy to take their place in the hall of fame. It is only necessary to mention such names as William Shrubsole, Stephen Elvey, Sir George Job Elvey, Herbert Stephen Irons, and Ethelbert William Bullinger, to realise what a nest of singing birds the old city contained, and Thomas Clark was one of the most famous of these.

The ancestors of Thomas Clark had been established in Canterbury for some generations. In the Marriage Register of St. Peters Church we find the following entry which records the marriage of his grand-father.

"1738 March 3rd, Thomas Clark, bachelor, and Mary White, spinster, both of this parish, by banns. Thomas Buttonshaw, Rector".

Thomas Clark was the Parish Clerk of St. Peters, and closely associated with the conduct of the services there.

The Register of Baptisms records that the Clark offspring began to arrive the next year but did not survive for very long. They were:

1. William   baptised December 16th 1739
   buried January 25th 1740.

2. Richard   baptised November 14th 1742
   buried January 24th 1743.

3. John   baptised March 4th 1743
   buried September 21st 1744.

4. William the last son was born posthumously and was not baptised at St. Peters.

Thomas Clark the Parish Clerk was buried at St. Peters June 15th 1745, but there is no indication that his wife was also buried there.

William the son of Thomas and Mary was duly apprenticed as a cordwainer. That is a boot-maker or a worker in leather.

Having served his apprenticeship William achieved the honour of becoming a Freeman of Canterbury in 1771.

St. Peters Church, St. Peters Street, Canterbury.

The record of his marriage is to be found in the register of St. Peters Church as follows "1774 January 25th, William Clark, bachelor, and Mary Quested, spinster, by Banns".

William then entered into business on his own account.

Very few of the many thousands who enter the premises of Messrs Marks & Spencer in Canterbury can realise that they are treading on historic ground.

One reason for interest in the building for modern generations is perhaps the fact that it was the only one in this area to survive the terrible blitz on the 1st June 1942.

To past generations however it was the site of No. 35 St. Georges Street or more familiarly known as Clark's Boot Shop.

The business of course derived its name from the fact that it belonged to Mr. William Clark, and it was here that his son Thomas was born in 1775. He was baptised in St. Peters Church, 5th February 1775.

The Clark family had become closely connected with the Wesleyan Methodist church where William was a member of the choir and also the choirmaster. The singing of the services was led by an orchestra, in which one of the relatives played the serpent.

With his father thus closely involved in church music the ears of little Thomas from a very early age were trained to appreciate the sacred strains. Moreover as the orchestra practised in the room behind the shop right under the little lad's bedroom he often found it difficult to go to sleep. Later the boy was regularly taken to choir practice where he soon learned the stirring music of Handel's oratorios. It is recorded of him that so proficient did he become in his mastry of the music, that when quite small he stood on a chair to conduct the choir and orchestra. At a very early age too he revealed an ability to compose hymn tunes. In fact long before he could read or write he mastered the art of putting the dots on the stave in grammatical order.

The sorrow of parting came to the home when Thomas was nineteen years old. The Kentish Register informs us that on January 6th 1794, Mrs. Clark wife of Mr. William Clark, shoe-maker, died in St. Georges Street, Canterbury. Her burial is recorded in the St. Peters Register, "1794 January 12th, Mary wife of William Clark, aged 55 years, from St. Georges Street in St. Georges Parish".

Almost on the anniversary of the burial of Mary, William married again to a woman much younger than himself. The service took place in St. Georges Church, just across the road from the shop, and the entry in the register is as follows "1795 January 14th, William Clark and Hannah Newman, both of this parish, by licence. Thomas Clark and Philip Penn, witnesses".

After just over another year death ended this second marriage, and Hannah was buried with Mary in St. Peters churchyard. The entry in the register is "1796 April 21st, Hannah wife of Mr. William Clark, Aged 37 years, from St. Georges Parish".

Thomas had been apprenticed to his father as a cordwainer. In 1796 he completed his term of service and was made a Freeman of Canterbury by reason of his birth.

At this period of his life Thomas travelled to every church possible in order to ring the bells. He is also recorded as ringing at Quex Park Birchington. His close friendship with

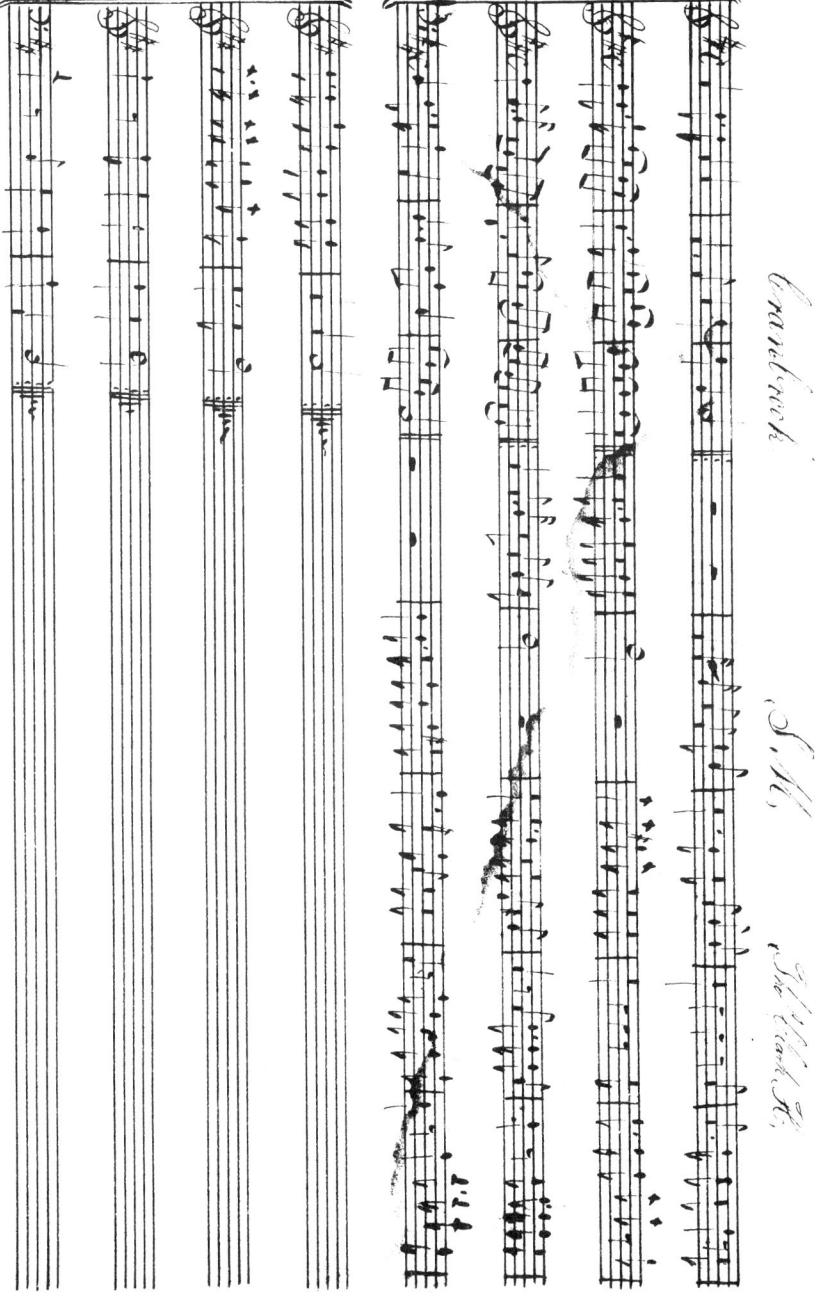

The original manuscript of "Cranbrook", signed by Thomas Clark.

the many members of the Francis family also encouraged him to travel to the scattered places where they lived. In particular he was frequently at Cranbrook, where with the aid of the youthful voices of the forty strong choir of Shepherds House School he was able to perfect many of his tunes. With the aid of John Francis, the master of that school, Thomas learned the art of reading and writing. This art he finally mastered at the age of twenty-eight.

His eminently singable tunes were in constant demand, not only by the choir of Cranbrook parish church, but from all over the south of England he received requests for tunes. As a compliment to those who appreciated his skill he named the tunes after the place for which he composed them.

The excellent training which he received at the hands of John Francis is reflected in the neatness with which his manuscript books were written. One such book which has survived is 12 x 9 x ¾, and it contains nine of the hymn tunes for which he afterwards became famous, and which are all signed by him. Namely, St. Peters, L.M., Cranbrook, S.M., Sunderland, S.M., Stanley, L.M., Weldon, C.M., Dunstable, P.M., Hadley, C.M., Rose Lane, C.M., and one he named Nativity. "St.Peters" was obviously named after the family church, "Cranbrook", after the home of his great friends, and "Rose Lane" after the little narrow lane which joined St. Georges Street with Watling Street but which, since it was blasted in the blitz, has become part of a wide thoroughfare. The book also contains six Psalm tunes which he composed, and five anthems, all good evidence of his skill and ability.

As his fame spread and the demand for his tunes increased the young composer was encouraged to go into print. This he did in 1805 when he was thirty years old.

This first collection of tunes was engraved by James Peck of 47 Lombard Street, London, and printed by Button, Whitaker & Beadnell, 75 St. Paul's Church Yard.

The title page is a beautiful example of the printers art, and not only did it set the standard for all future publications from the same source, but also used for the first time the form of ascription which distinguished the composer from any other man with a similar name. "Thomas Clark of Canterbury".

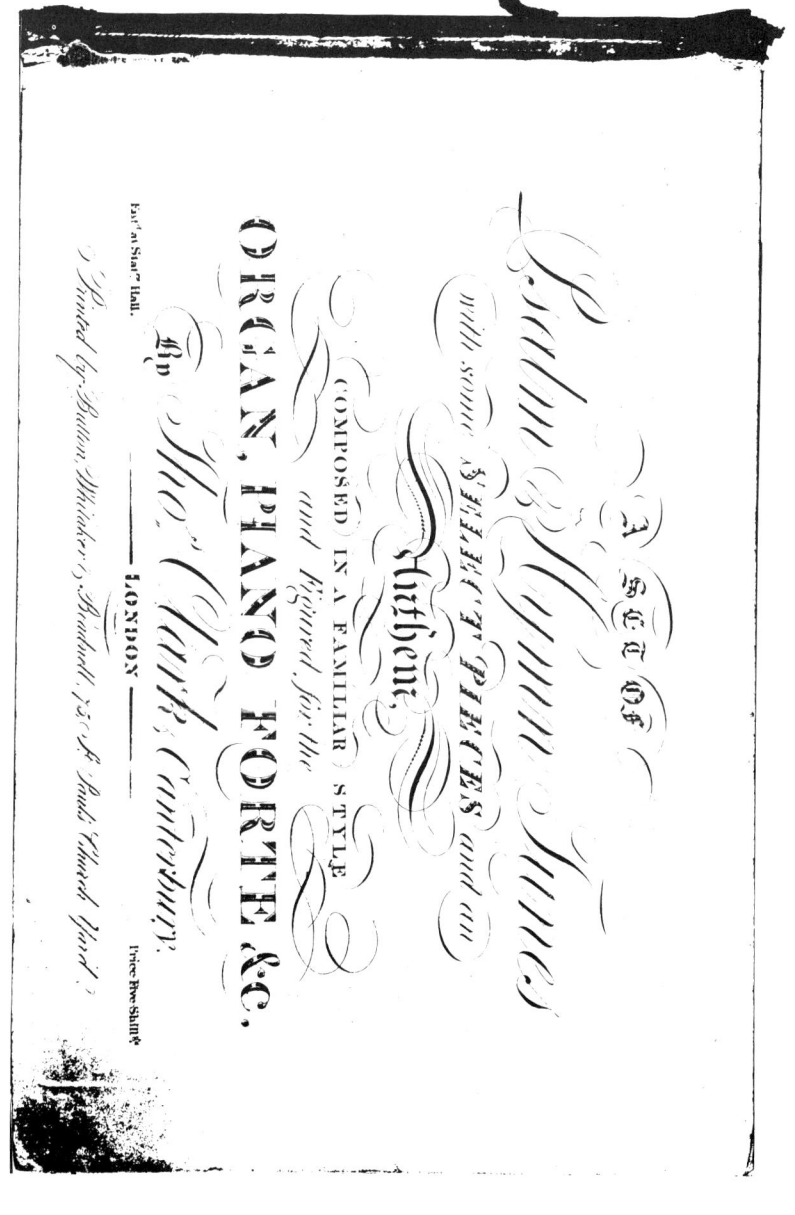

Title page from the "First Set of Psalm & Hymn Tunes", published in 1805.

Among the tunes which thus appeared in print for the first time were the already famous Cranbrook, Cornhill, and Burnham.

Here we find Cranbrook firmly wedded to Philip Doddridge's hymn "Grace 'tis a charming sound, Harmonious to the ear". A happy union which was preserved in the hymn books of all denominations even to the present day.

The rousing tune "Cornhill" was composed for Isaac Watt's hymn, "Raise your triumphant songs, To an immortal tune", and in its day it achieved great popularity.

An interesting story has been preserved of the origin of the tune "Burnham". After Elizabeth Oliver, nee Francis, had left Winchelsea to go and live in Greater Watering, Essex, her brother Jabez and Thomas Clark went to stay with her. While there the two young men entered into a friendly competition to see who could compose a tune the quickest. Jabez Francis named his tune "Winchelsea" after the old home of his sister, and Thomas Clark named his "Burnham" after the local seaside town. Clark composed it for Wesley's hymn, "Ye virgin souls arise, With all the dead awake", but future generations preferred to sing it to "Rejoice the Lord is King; Your Lord and King adore".

The whole Set contains twenty-seven tunes and one anthem, "Hear my prayer O God".

This "First Set of Psalm and Hymn Tunes" met with immediate success, and in the autumn of that year Clark was encouraged to publish "An Ode to the New Year", which began with the pompous words, "Stand still reflugent orb". This ode was published by James Peck of Lombard Street, London.

Encouraged by the outstanding success of his first venture into print Thomas Clark produced his "Second Set of Psalm and Hymn Tunes", with some select pieces composed in a familiar style and figured for the organ, pianoforte etc., in 1806. This Set was again engraved by James Peck, but the name of the printer was changed to John Whitaker & Co., 75 St. Pauls Church Yard. This Set contained thirty-seven new tunes, none of which seem to have attained immortality. Either the sopranos of those days had a higher range than their modern counterparts or were more willing to try to sing the high notes, for most of the tunes in this Set flourish with top Fs and Gs.

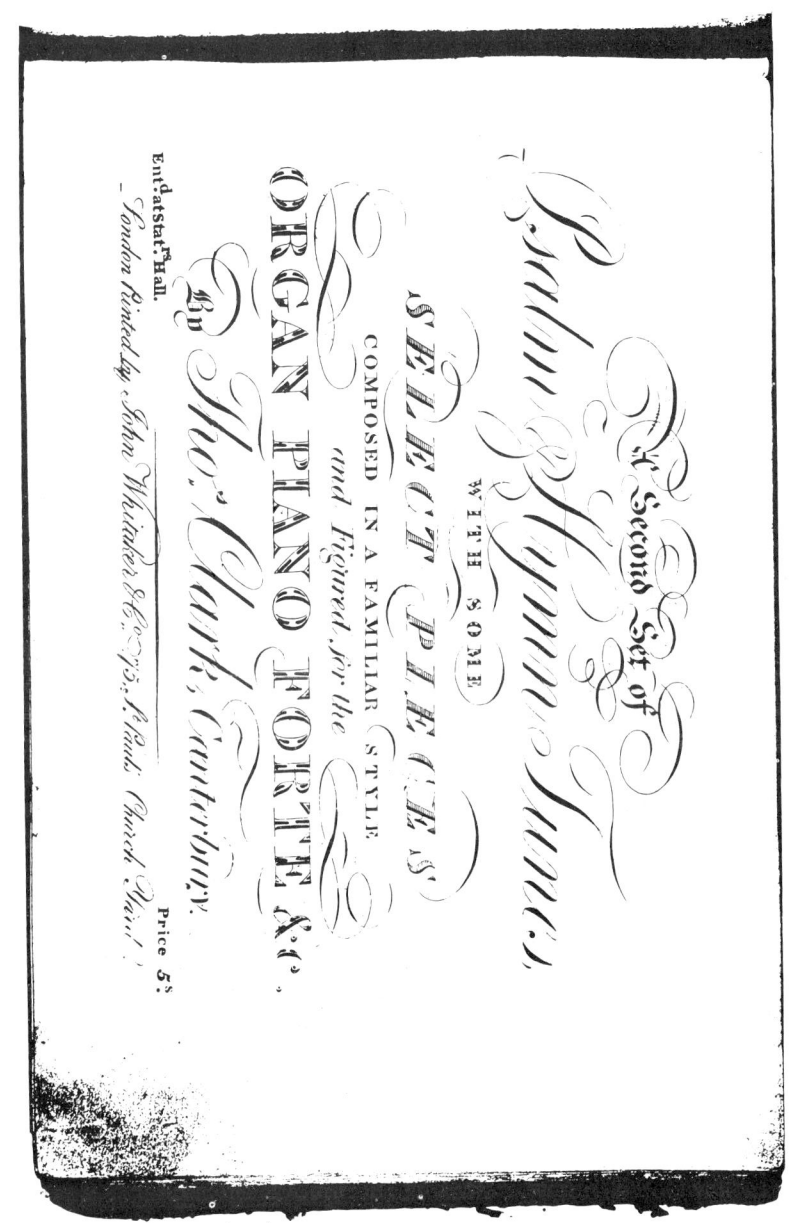

Title page from the "Second Set of Psalm & Hymn Tunes", published in 1806.

This Second Set was closely followed by the production by the same publishers of "A Sett of Psalm Tunes with Symphonies and an Instrumental Bass, adapted for the use of Parish or Country Choirs and figured for the organ etc."

In an advertisement published with the Second Set of Psalm and Hymn Tunes Clark expresses his intention, "that should the work meet with the approbation of the public as generally as his previous works, it would be his endeavour to merit the continuance of the same liberal encouragement in the publication of a Third Set of Psalm and Hymn Tunes".

The necessary encouragement being forthcoming, the "Third Set of Psalm and Hymn Tunes" duly made its appearance in 1807. The Set contains thirty-six new tunes, one of which, "Warsaw", Clark composed for Philip Doddridge's hymn, "Loud to the Prince of Heaven your cheerful voices raise". In the present Methodist Hymn Book it is sung with equal pleasure to Wesley's, "Come, all whoe'er have set your faces Zion-ward".

The ever increasing circulation of his earlier works now enabled Clark to advertise a reduction in price both for quarto and folio editions.

"Clark's First Set of Psalm & Hymn Tunes 4/6d.

Clark's Second Set of Psalm & Hymn Tunes 5/0d. Quarto.

Clark's First Set of Psalm Tunes 4/6d.

Clark's Second Set of Psalm Tunes 5/0d. Folio."

It will be seen from this advertisement that Clark had published a Second Set of Psalm Tunes in 1807, but it has not been possible to trace a copy.

With the Third Set of Psalm and Hymn Tunes Thomas Clark announced that "The very favourable reception which the Composers preceding works have experienced induce him to intimate his intention to publish "A Fourth Set of Psalm and Hymn Tunes".

It was however not until 1810 that the Fourth Set duly appeared. In this instance it was printed for the Author and sold by James Peck No. 47 Lombard Street, Messrs. Williams and Smith, Stationers Court, and Messrs. Button and Whitaker, St. Pauls Church Yard. This may indicate that for some reason his usual publishers were reluctant to act for him and that he was therefore compelled to publish it at his own expense.

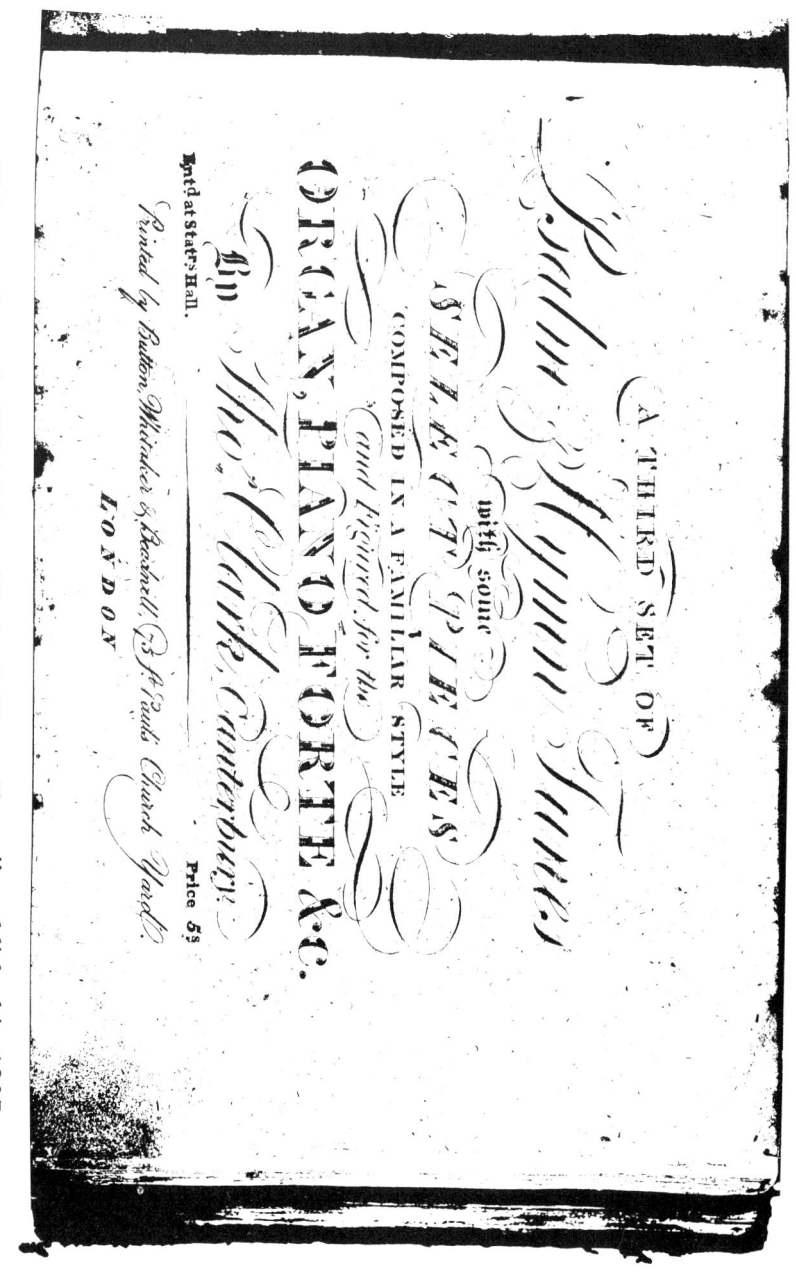

Title page from the "Third Set of Psalm & Hymn Tunes", published in 1807.

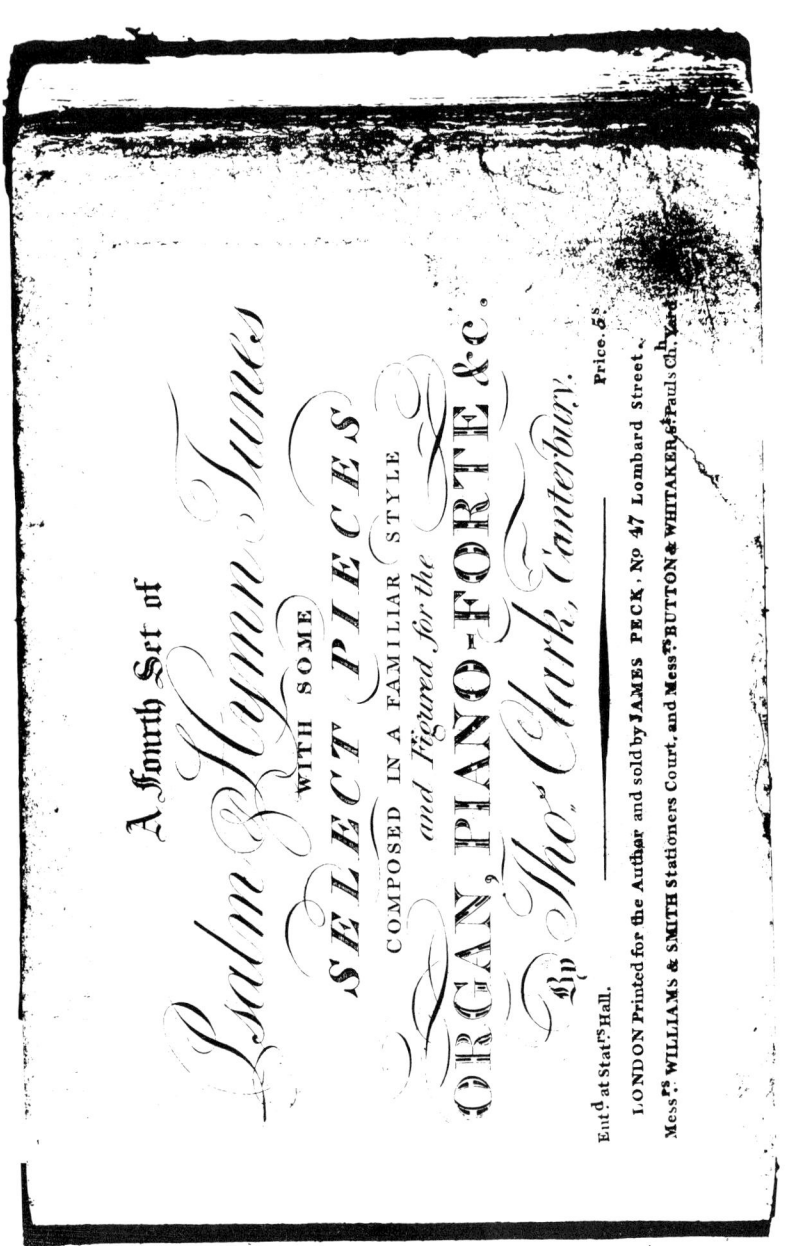

Title page from the "Fourth Set of Psalm & Hymn Tunes", published in 1810.

Title page from the "Fifth Set of Psalm & Hymn Tunes", published in 1811.

This Fourth Set of Psalm and Hymn Tunes contained thirty-four new tunes, one of which was composed for words written by Mr. William Kingsford of Canterbury entitled "The Happy Man".

Another interesting example of Clark's art is the tune "Salvation", which he composed for Isaac Watt's "Salvation O the joyful sound". The verse "Salvation let the echo fly" he arranged for full chorus, first and second violins, first and second tenors, first and second altos, first and second bass, soprano and organ. One can well imagine the effect of this when sung with the vigour of full heart and voice.

During this year Clark published a new edition of his works at his own expense. Published by the author:

Quarto, Psalm & Hymn Tunes, Three Books, each 5s.

Folio, Psalm Tunes with Symphonies, Two Books each 5s.

With the Fourth Set of Psalm and Hymn Tunes Clark announced "The author respectfully begs permission to return sincere thanks for the very favourable manner in which his compositions have been received; from the unexpected success of which, he is induced to announce his intention to commence very shortly, a new Set of Tunes and Pieces, to be published in twelve monthly numbers." This project was duly carried out, and each part was sold for 1/0d.

In 1811 Thomas Clark produced his "Fifth Set of Psalm and Hymn Tunes". The title page informs us that it was printed for Button, Whitaker, and Beadnell, 75 St. Pauls Church Yard. Although there is no statement to the effect it may be presumed that it was published by the author. This was the largest work so far produced by the author, and it included an anthem composed especially for the opening of a new chapel at Maidstone, and also an anthem the words for which were written by Mr. William Kingsford of Canterbury. Apart from the two pieces mentioned this Fifth Set contained ninety-one new tunes.

During this period of his life Clark appears to have been closely engaged in his business, and musical affairs around Canterbury. In April 1811 the Wesleyan Methodists purchased a site for a new chapel on the Island of Binnewith, and the stone-laying ceremony took place on Tuesday 7th May 1811. Although Thomas Clark's name does not appear in the official records it is a well established tradition that he was at this

The Methodist Church, St. Peters Street, Canterbury.

time engaged to take charge of the singers and to write special music for the opening of the new chapel. The new chapel was opened on Wednesday 1st January 1812. In his book, "The Music of the Methodist Hymn-Book" James T. Lightwood states of Clark that, "For many years he was the leader of the Methodist Choir at Canterbury, and many special musical services were held there under his direction". It would indeed appear that this was the case and that Thomas Clark directed the music there until William Warman, a schoolmaster of 38 St. Peters Street, was appointed "leader of the singers" in 1841.

It is possible that about this time William Clark either retired from the business or died, as his name does not appear to be associated with St. Georges Street and does not appear in the poll books. If he was indeed the William Clark living in North Lane in 1835, he would have been about 89 years old then.

From all accounts it is certain that Thomas Clark was very much engaged in Canterbury and the surrounding villages during the next three years. His help was eagerly sought after for chapel and Sunday School anniversaries, and his presence was considered to ensure both a good sing and a good congregation.

Despite a very busy life Clark managed to find time to produce in 1812 a "Sixth Set of Hymn Tunes". This Set contained fifty new tunes and was published by James Peck.

The Public had to wait until 1815 for the appearance of Clark's next work, which was published by Messrs. Button and Whitaker under the title of a "Fifth Set of Psalm Tunes and Two Anthems with Symphonies and an Instrumental Bass". Also four chants composed and adapted for the use of country choirs.

It is quite possible that the strains and stresses of the Napoleonic wars may have made it difficult for Clark to produce more works at that time, but another five years were to elapse before the stream started to flow again.

All was not happy at St. Peters Methodist Church, for in July 1816 the Leaders Meeting passed the following strong resolution. "In consequence of the indevout and improper behaviour of some persons in our Singing Gallery, during the solemn worship of Almighty God, in future no person who is not a member of the Methodist Society (except the organist) shall sit in the Singing Gallery without the approbation of a Leaders Meeting".

This resolution may or may not have applied to Clark, but there is no evidence that he was a member of the Society at that time. However the resolution did not appear to have the desired effect, but produced something in the nature of a demonstration.

In September a special meeting of the Leaders was held under the chairmanship of the District Chairman, John Gaulter, when an even stronger resolution was passed, as follows:

"1st. No person shall be admitted into the orchestra as a singer, who lives in habitual, open sin.

2nd. No person shall be permitted to retain his seat in the orchestra whose behaviour is irreverent during divine service.

3rd. All persons who after their admission as singers fall

into acts of immorality shall be subject to an expulsion from the orchestra.

4th. No person shall be admitted to, or retain his seat in the orchestra, who refuses subordination to the committee appointed by this meeting to superintend the orchestra."

Despite this seemingly depraved state of affairs Methodism continued to extend its influence, notably in Whitstable, six miles to the north, where cottage meetings had been held since 1802, and from 1812 a company had walked to Canterbury every Sunday for service. The Rev. James Bromley, who was second minister in 1816–1817, brought about a number of conversions, and although he left for Margate the revival continued, with the result that a chapel was built and opened at Whitstable in 1819. The revival continued through the winter of 1820–1821, when in one month there were between fifty and sixty conversions.

What part Clark played in this revival, if any, is a case for speculation, but he found time in 1820 to produce a "Sixth Set of Psalm Tunes with a Morning and Evening Hymn". This was published by Messrs. Button and Whitaker.

This was closely followed in the same year by a "Seventh Set of Hymn Tunes, being a Set of new tunes, the poetry selected from Dr. Collyer's Hymn Book, composed in a familiar style and figured for the organ, pianoforte etc." Many of the tunes contained in this Set were readily appropriated by a number of denominations.

In 1820 there also appeared "Walker's Companion to Dr. Rippon's Tune Book, fifth edition". This was printed for and sold by T. Walker, 25 Red Lion Street, Spital Square. This was the standard tune book of the St. Georges Baptist Church in Canterbury at that period, the Singing Gallery copy of which was rebound in 1836. A most curious note appears in the advertisement to the effect that "Cranbrook, Margate, and Parting, are put into this volume with the consent of Mr. Peck". Cranbrook and Parting are both marked as being private property, and Margate as never before having been published. This is strange as there is no other information that Mr. Peck had purchased the copyright or why his personal permission should have been given for their publication. As for the claim that Margate had never before been published, it must have been a well-known fact that it was first published in the Third Set of Psalm and Hymn Tunes, in 1807. Sangate which appeared in 1806 in the Second Set of Psalm and Hymn Tunes is duly ascribed to Clark, but such a well-known tune as Calcutta is not credited to anyone.

The next work which the composer produced would appear to have been the "Sacred Gleaner". As this was not published until 1830 it would seem that Clark had been somewhat inactive during the past ten years. However it was published by William Blackman, 5 Bridge Street, Borough, London, and sold for 12/0d. or in three parts at 5/0d. each.

James T. Lightwood says that this work achieved a large circulation, and great popularity. It was, he affirms, a standard set of tunes with many congregations.

In December 1831 Clark composed an anthem which was destined to become very popular. It was entitled, "God came from Teman", and it was published by William Blackman, 5 Bridge Street, Borough. At this time in his life the composer regularly produced anthems which were sold at 1/0d. each. Lightwood has recorded that, "One of his anthems, 'Daughter of Zion', achieved an extraordinary popularity, and the crashing chord at the end of the phrase, 'chariots of war', is ever a joyful memory to those who have heard or sung it".

Thomas Clark does not appear to have produced any major work during the next six years, and then in 1837 the Sunday School Union decided to engage him to compile a collection of tunes, which was known as the Union Tune Book, and was destined to establish Clark's fame for many years to come. The collection was duly published by the Sunday School Union, and it contained thirty eight of Clark's tunes and the Union Introduction to Singing. With reference to this the Preface states that "It has been prepared with a view to assist those who wish to acquire a sufficient knowledge of the science to sing the praises of God correctly". The Committee, in publishing this work, expressed the hope that it would supply a collection of agreeable and useful tunes, which, without departing from the style of music appropriate to devotional feelings, should yet contain such a variety as would be adapted to religious exercises in general. The work contained three hundred and nineteen tunes, of which Clark contributed thirty-eight, some of which had been published

"Cranbrook" — a page from the first edition of "The Union Tune Book", published in 1837.

THE UNION INTRODUCTION TO SINGING.

PRELIMINARY REMARKS.

(ADDRESSED TO LEARNERS.)

THIS "Introduction to Singing" has been prepared with a view to assist those who wish to acquire a sufficient knowledge of the science to sing the praises of God correctly; and also to encourage the cultivation of vocal music in schools. The following remarks are addressed to beginners.

The learner, if unable to procure the instruction of a professional teacher, need not be discouraged: he may probably obtain some assistance from a friend who understands music. But if not, he may still proceed; for, by patient application, he will soon overcome many apparent difficulties.

A beginner ought not to proceed too quickly. He should thoroughly learn the characters used in music, and fix them in his memory by writing out a copy of them.

The management of the voice requires great attention. To produce full mellow tones, the sound should proceed freely from the chest, and the mouth be opened moderately, with the appearance of a smile. Do not sing loudly at first; for the voice will assuredly be injured by being strained: select that part for which your voice is most adapted. Practise the sounds of the notes in the scale, both ascending and descending, as far as the voice can be extended without forcing it. Let the voice dwell firmly on each sound; begin moderately, gradually increase the sound till the middle, and then decrease until it die away. By thus practising the sounds in the scale, which many might do whilst at their daily occupations, the voice will be materially strengthened and improved.

Singers ought to pronounce the words distinctly and accurately. The sounds of the vowels must be carefully attended to. The hissing sound of the letters *s* and *c* should be passed over lightly, especially when it occurs at the end of a line. Every one will allow that the *words* are the most important part of sacred music: *they* ought therefore to be sung in a feeling and expressive manner.

All such bad habits as singing through the nose, distorting the face, beginning lines abruptly, making a loud noise, taking breath

THE UNION INTRODUCTION TO SINGING.

in the middle of a word, and dwelling too long on the last note, are very disagreeable, and ought to be carefully avoided. On the contrary, you should endeavour to sing with ease, and with a pleasant countenance. The attitude of the body is also worthy of some attention: standing is the best position; but whether standing or sitting, the body should be gracefully erect.

Those persons who lead the singing should be careful to select tunes adapted to the words. A hymn expressive of joy and praise ought to be set to a tune of the same character; on the other hand, a tune of a plaintive cast will best suit a hymn expressing grief or prayer. Some tunes, such as IRISH, No. 5, may be sung quicker or slower according to the words: these will suit hymns expressing varied emotions. The leader should not choose a tune which requires the repetition of some of the words in a line, unless he wish to give emphasis to these particular words. On no account should he set a tune to words which would be broken and mutilated by the repetition of the music; and, to guard against this evil, before fixing on a tune in which the lines, or parts of them, are repeated, he should carefully look through all the verses. Devotional feeling has been greatly hindered, and sacred music has frequently been rendered ridiculous by carelessness in this respect.

In concluding these observations, the reader is reminded that there are many encouragements in the Holy Scriptures, which should animate us to aim at excellence in the delightful exercise of singing praises to God. The example of the Old Testament saints—the fact that our blessed Redeemer himself joined with his disciples in singing a hymn, Matt. xxvi. 30—the injunctions of the apostles, Eph. v. 19, Col. iii. 16, James v. 13, together with their example, and that of their followers, Acts xvi. 25*, should stimulate us to improvement in this heavenly art, while we should be especially careful also to enter into the spirit of this sacred devotional employment. There are none of the engagements of the saints on earth of which we can say with so much certainty that they will be perpetuated in heaven, as this delightful one of praising God. Reader, may you be one of " the ransomed of the Lord," who " shall return, and come to " the heavenly " Zion with songs and everlasting joy upon their heads;" who " shall obtain joy and gladness, and sorrow and sighing shall" for ever " flee away." Amen.

---

* In Pliny's Letters to Trajan, the early Christians are accused of meeting together " to sing hymns to Christ as God."

before, and some which were new. Immediate success rewarded this publication, and by an ever increasing demand the public showed its sincere appreciation of the compiler and the esteem with which it regarded his work.

The Committee of the Sunday School Union announced that they were most gratified to find from the extensive sale of the Union Tune Book, that their opinion as to the necessity of such a work was well founded.

We now move on to the year 1841 when the Committee of the Sunday School Union announced that in the preparation of the Union Tune Book many pieces had been laid aside, which from their length and the greater difficulty of the music, were considered as not adapted for general use.

The Committee therefore felt encouraged to publish a collection of sacred music of a more elevated character. Once again they sought the valuable assistance of Thomas Clark of Canterbury, with the result that in 1841 they were able to publish the Union Harmonist. In the Preface they pointed out that it was obvious that music of this description would require more attention than ordinary psalmody, but it was hoped and in fact believed that Sunday School teachers partook of the increasing disposition to cultivate vocal harmony, and that they would feel little difficulty in making themselves acquainted with the compositions then selected. The Preface further informs us that the greater number of the pieces were arranged by Mr. T. Clark of Canterbury, to whose zeal and talent in the discharge of the duty undertaken by him, the Committee felt much pleasure in bearing public testimony.

Having thus assured the musical education and interest of the adult congregations and Sunday School teachers, the Sunday School Union next turned its attention to the juveniles, and Thomas Clark was once again the obvious choice for compiler. With undiminished energy he carried out his task and thereby enabled the Sunday School Union to publish the Juvenile Harmonist in 1842. The Preface informs us that the Committee of the Sunday School Union published the Union Harmonist and the Union Tune Book with the professed design to aid the efforts in progress for the improvement of singing in Christian congregations and Sunday Schools. While engaged in these attempts, they were not

THE UNION TUNE BOOK,

A Selection of Psalm and Hymn Tunes,

SUITABLE FOR USE IN CONGREGATIONS AND SUNDAY SCHOOLS.

ARRANGED BY THOMAS CLARK,
OF CANTERBURY.

LONDON:
SUNDAY SCHOOL UNION,
60, PATERNOSTER ROW.

Title page from "The Union Tune Book", published in 1841.

THE
UNION HARMONIST,

A SELECTION OF SACRED MUSIC,

CONSISTING OF ORIGINAL AND STANDARD PIECES, ANTHEMS, &c.

SUITABLE FOR USE IN SUNDAY SCHOOLS, CONGREGATIONS, AND MUSICAL SOCIETIES.

ARRANGED BY THOMAS CLARK, OF CANTERBURY.

LONDON:

SUNDAY SCHOOL UNION, No. 60, PATERNOSTER ROW.

1841.

Title page from "The Union Harmonist", published in 1841.

THE
JUVENILE HARMONIST,

A SELECTION OF

Tunes and Pieces for Children.

ARRANGED FOR TWO TREBLES AND A BASS

By T. CLARK OF CANTERBURY.

SUNDAY SCHOOL UNION,

56, OLD BAILEY, LONDON, E.C.

Title page from "The Juvenile Harmonist", published in 1842.

unmindful that children had a special claim upon them for a supply of vocal music, of a sacred and also of a cheerful character, and they have accordingly published, in a cheap and convenient form, a collection of attractive tunes and pieces, which are peculiarly adapted to youthful voices and youthful feelings.

This collection, as now presented for the use of the young both in families and schools, consists of eighty-seven tunes and pieces intended for devotional exercises in Sunday Schools; and sixty-one tunes and pieces adapted to moral and descriptive words, designed for familiar practice during the week; arranged for three voices — two trebles and a bass — by Mr. Thomas Clark, of Canterbury.

Apart from the eleven tunes which formed his own personal contribution to the work, Clark introduced to the children for the first time that delightful and well loved tune Infant Praise, set to the words "Children of Jerusalem," and that equally well loved hymn by young Jemima Thompson "I think when I read that sweet story of old" which she had written during the previous year. The hymn of course, as then used by Clark only consisted of two verses, as the third verse was not written until 1853.

Clark's fame and popularity continued to increase by leaps and bounds, his works were in ever increasing demand. The continued popularity of the Union Tune Book, and the receipt of some interesting communications suggesting improvements, induced the Committee to undertake a careful revision of the entire book and the selection of additional tunes, in order to render it more acceptable and complete. Mr. Thomas Clark of Canterbury was once again engaged to carry out this important task and to re-harmonize the tunes. The greatly improved edition was duly completed and published in 1842. Thirty-seven of the tunes contained in the first edition were omitted and their places filled by others suited to the advancing state of musical knowledge, fifty-two tunes being likewise added, which increased the total number to three hundred and seventy-one. Many of these additional tunes adapted to hymns of peculiar metres were expressly composed for the work by the Editor.

THE UNION TUNE BOOK,

A SELECTION OF PSALM AND HYMN TUNES,

SUITABLE FOR USE IN CONGREGATIONS AND SUNDAY SCHOOLS.

ARRANGED BY THOMAS CLARK, OF CANTERBURY.

LONDON:
SUNDAY SCHOOL UNION, No. 60, PATERNOSTER ROW.
1843.

Title page from "The Union Tune Book", published in 1843.

The variety thus being extended so as to include forty-three different metres, of these Clark's own personal contribution was thirty-six tunes. Such was the unprecedented demand for the work, that the next year, in order to place the music within reach of all, the Sunday School Union published a portable edition by the omission of the pianoforte accompaniment, with the most gratifying results.

The outstanding success of this work seems to have encouraged Clark on to a great burst of production in 1843. Writing from Canterbury on the 16th February, 1843, Thomas Clark said that "while numerous compilations had been published, he was not aware that any one composer had hitherto set the whole of the Psalms to music. With himself it had long been a favourite object, and though in imperfect strains, he had thus rendered his homage to the 'sweet singer of Israel,' it would prove to him a source of peculiar satisfaction, should the manner in which he had fulfilled his task, meet with the approval of the Christian Public." He continued "that if a certain degree of monotony is discoverable, it must in extenuation be remarked that neither the metre nor the subject had allowed of that variety which is attainable in promiscuous selection; the words having been taken exclusively from the Old and New Versions and Dr. Watts. That the utility of the work might not be restricted, and as words equally appropriate could be selected from the hymn books in general use, the metre, with a distinctive name had been attached to each tune, while for the convenience of the Organist a figured bass had been introduced." This most interesting work was published by J. Hart, 109 Hatton Garden, under the title of David's Harp, a series of original tunes composed expressly to The Psalter by Thomas Clark of Canterbury, and sold for 8/0d., or in six parts at 1/6d. each. By this means one hundred and fifty very useful and singable tunes were presented to the public.

PART I	PSALMS 1–24	PART IV	PSALMS 73–96
PART II	PSALMS 25–48	PART V	PSALMS 97–120
PART III	PSALMS 49–72	PART VI	PSALMS 121–150

For some years, William Blackman of 5 Bridge Street Borough had published anthems in twos and threes and sold each number for 1/0d. Many of these anthems were written

DAVID'S HARP:

A SERIES OF ORIGINAL TUNES,

COMPOSED EXPRESSLY TO

The Psalter;

BY THOMAS CLARK,

CANTERBURY.

LONDON: J. HART, 109, HATTON GARDEN.

Price Eight Shillings, Cloth, or in six Parts, at One Shilling and Sixpence each.

Title page from "David's Harp", published in 1843.

by Thomas Clark, who selected sixty-one of the best examples and published them in three volumes. Eventually in 1843 they were bound in one volume and sold for £1. 4s. 0d. Of these pieces, twenty-nine were contributed by Clark, and included among other interesting examples, an anthem "Salvation" arranged for a flute, two violins, two altos, two tenors and two basses, also a popular anthem "God came from Teman," which he had composed in December, 1831. The beautiful steel engraved title page, complete with heavenly cherubs, trumpeter and harpist, gives the title of the work as The Seraphim or Sacred Harmonist, a collection of original and select pieces, anthems etc., from the most esteemed authors, arranged for the use of congregations, choirs and societies, with an accompaniment for the organ or pianoforte, by Thomas Clark of Canterbury.

During the past years Thomas Clark had been engaged in compiling a collection of tunes for the use of the Congregationalists. This was now published in four volumes under the title of The Congregational Harmonist or Clerk's Companion. A numerous selection of the most approved Psalm and Hymn tunes of standard reputation with many originals, comprising a great variety of measures suitable to the collections of Dr. Watts, Rippon, Collyer, Mr. R. Hill, Mr. Wesley and Lady Huntingdon. The whole selected, arranged, composed and figured for the organ or pianoforte by W. Blackman, 5 Bridge Street Borough and sold, price 7/6d. each volume boards, half bound 8/6d. As an example of the widespread market for the works of Thomas Clark, it is of interest to note that this work might also be obtained from Dalmaine and Co., Soho Square, Simpkin and Marshal Stationers Court; Wood and Co., Edinburgh, Alday Dublin, and of all music and booksellers.

Unfortunately, it has not been possible to trace and inspect a copy of either volumes one or two, but as volume three begins at number three hundred and ninety, we may gather some conception of the size of the previous volumes. Volume three however, contains one hundred and eighty-three pieces of which forty-two are by Clark, while volume four contains one hundred and ninety-two of which Clark wrote sixty-eight.

Title page from "The Seraphim or Sacred Harmonist", published in 1843.

THE
CONGREGATIONAL HARMONIST,
Or Clerk's Companion,

A numerous Selection of the most approved Psalm and Hymn Tunes,
OF STANDARD REPUTATION,
WITH

MANY ORIGINALS.

Comprising a great Variety of Measures, suitable to the Collections of
Drs. WATTS, RIPPON, COLLYER, Mr. R. HILL, Mr. WESLEY, LADY HUNTINGDON, &c.

THE WHOLE SELECTED, ARRANGED, COMPOSED, AND FIGURED FOR THE

Organ or Piano Forte.

IN FOUR VOLUMES.

By T. CLARK,
Canterbury.

Vol.   Pr.

Price ea: 7s. 6d. boards, Half Bound 8s. 6d.

London, Published for the Editor by W. BLACKMAN, 5, Bridge Street, Borough, where may be had, the SACRED GLEANER complete, 12s. half bound, or in three parts stitched singly, 5s. each; may likewise be had of DALMAINE and Co. Soho Square; SIMPKIN and MARSHALL, Stationers' Court; WOOD and Co. Edinburgh; ALDAY, Dublin; and of all Music and Booksellers.
Two Volumes strongly half bound in calf 15s.

Title page from "The Congregational Harmonist or Clerk's Companion", published in 1843.

THE

UNION TUNE BOOK,

A Selection of Tunes and Chants,

SUITABLE FOR USE IN CONGREGATIONS AND
SUNDAY SCHOOLS.

ARRANGED BY T. CLARK, AND J. I. COBBIN.

TREBLE AND BASS PARTS.

LONDON:
SUNDAY SCHOOL UNION:
56, OLD BAILEY, E.C.

Title page from "The Union Tune Book", published in 1854.

Additional to this work, a new edition of the Sacred Gleaner with a supplement was published, thereby forming an Appendix to the Congregational Harmonist, the whole work comprising one thousand tunes and pieces. Among the tunes thus published were Ticmore End, Francis, Shortwood, Nailsworth and Uley, which were specially composed and inserted in this work at the particular request of Mr. B. F. Flint, for hymns having been written by his maternal grandfather, the late Rev. B. Francis, who was upwards of forty years Pastor of the Baptist Church at Shortwood near Horsley Green, Gloucestershire.

This glorious musical activity for the year 1843 was to represent virtually the crowning effort of Clark's sixty-eight years of life. During the next few years he was to retire from his busy shop in St. George's Street to the comparative calm of Stour Street. Moreover, a drastic change was to take place in his spiritual life. After years of service as choirmaster at St. Peter's Wesleyan Church, since its opening in 1811, he severed his connection and left to join the General Baptists at the Black Friars.

Since the publication of the improved edition of the Union Tune Book in 1842, a greatly improved musical taste had been created. In the words of the Committee, an unprecedented popular movement on the subject of vocal music had taken place. The Union, desiring to foster this improvement and advancement of sacred music, decided yet once again to engage Thomas Clark — who with the assistance of Mr. J. I. Cobbin, who was appointed editor, compiled a continuation to the Union Tune Book. They were instructed by the Committee to furnish a collection of tunes suitable to the present times rather than attempt a revision of the former selection. Although the editorship was officially entrusted to Mr. J. I. Cobbin, prior credit was given to Thomas Clark for his valuable efforts in arranging the music. This Continuation to the Union Tune Book was published in June 1854. It contained one hundred and ten tunes, of which Clark contributed eight, and thirty-seven chants which included a double chant by the compiler.

With his removal to Stour Street, the sands of time continued to run out very quietly for Thomas Clark. Although his days of publishing music had past, he remained an important personality in the world of church music. His elevating tunes passed into the collections of all denominations, including even the Roman Catholics. Moreover, he continued to be in great demand at church anniversaries over the whole of East Kent, travelling from place to place in a friend's dog-cart. James T. Lightwood has recorded the memories of an old Cathedral Chorister who knew Clark personally. Treasured memories of "Sunday evening sings" organized by Clark throughout the declining years of his life. Truly it was an outstanding life which was a shining example of how a man could, by his own efforts, overcome lack of birth, riches, education and social position, and rise to command the respect and gratitude of countless thousands of his fellow men. His dedicated skill produced worthy boots and shoes for the people of East Kent, while his intellect was continually used to make, not only his neighbours, but people in many countries, including America, sing as they had never done before.

The Kentish Gazette of the period, informs us that he died in his home, St. Mildreds, Canterbury, on May 30th, 1859, aged 84 years.

He was Laid to Rest in the unconsecrated portion of the Wincheap Burial Ground, in grave No 95, on the 3rd June 1859.

Entrance to Wincheap Burial Ground, Canterbury.

Throughout all his long life he had unsparingly dedicated his time and talents to help the Spiritual Revolution which accompanied the Industrial Revolution. He lived in and through a time of great difficulty and change, and did much to bridge the vast chasm between the rich and the poor. By his inspiring tunes, his compositions and his personal influence he infused hope to many a failing heart. Yet in all his successes, he never failed to share his honour with his native city. Proud of his Freedom, the son of a Freeman, he was a son of whom his mother city might justly be proud and grateful. Grateful, not only for the legacy of music created by his skill, but also that he never failed to share his honour with his birthplace, and always proudly signed himself,

Thomas Clark of Canterbury.

CRANBROOK AND ITS TUNE

In these modern days, when mankind is slowly awakening to the value to be placed on the treasures of past ages, Cranbrook, that charming old world town in the Weald of Kent, may justly claim to have pride of place. Despite the inevitable changes wrought by the hand of time, this beautiful little town has retained much of its old world charm, its quaint timber buildings, and evidences of its long eventful history. The modern inhabitants look back with pride to the time when king Edward III established the profitable woollen industry there, and encouraged many Flemish craftsmen to come and settle there. Broadcloth halls were soon built and the place reached a high state of prosperity by the time Queen Elizabeth visited the town in 1573.

This historic country town, nestling beside the pleasant little river Crane, in the charming undulating Kentish countryside, still has much to offer not only to the lover of the historic past, but also to those interested in the progressive present.

On either side of the High Street, and the narrower Stone Street, which joints it at right-angles, may be seen many survivals of interesting examples of English domestic architecture. The old Town Hall, the almost cathedral-like parish church of St. Dunstan, the many timber framed buildings, and the famous mill, all add their attractive charm to the place. The mill which dominates the view at one end of the town, was built in 1814, at a cost of £3,500, and it is considered to be one of the most perfect specimens to have survived to the present day.

The story of how this notable place came to have an equally famous hymn tune named after it is gripping in interest.

About the year 1928, an old Yorkshire schoolmaster established the fact that the words of the well-known folk song, "On Ilkley Moor baht 'at", were composed by the conductor of the Heptonstall Glee Choir, and were sung by that choir for the first time in 1877, to Thomas Clark's famous tune Cranbrook.

Cranbrook, Stone Street.

This curious marriage of word and tune achieved an outstanding popularity, and firmly established it as a Yorkshire folk song.

The words of the song, almost inane in their poverty of conception, as printed in the popular song books are:

1. Wheear 'as tha been sin' ah saw thee?
   On Ilkley Moor baht 'at.
2. Tha's been a coortin Mary Jane.
3. Tha'll go and get thi deeath o'cowld.
4. Then we shall ha' to bury thee.
5. Then t'worms'll come an' ate thee up.
6. Then t'ducks'll come an' ate up t'worms.
7. Then we shall go an' ate up t'ducks.
8. Then we shall all 'ave etten thee.
9. That's wheear we get our oahn back.

Although folk songs are the product of the common people, for the common people to sing, it is obvious that this song must rely for its success and popularity on the tune to which it is so firmly wedded.

Even a cursory search through the hymn tune books of our grand-fathers will establish the fact that this popular folk tune is none other than the famous hymn tune Cranbrook, composed by Thomas Clark of St. Georges Street, Canterbury, and published for the first time in his First Set of Psalm and Hymn Tunes, in 1805.

The tune Cranbrook owes not only its name but also much of its subsequent success to the association of Thomas Clark with the Francis family of that place.

The pedigree of the Francis family may with profit be traced back to the Rev. John Francis M.A., who was instituted vicar of Lympne in Kent on June 20th 1610, but resigned in 1616, and was instituted vicar of Ripple near Dover on September 23rd 1616.

The various branches of the family undoubtedly inherited from their distinguished ancestor many of his talents besides his strong Protestant principles. During his incumbancy of the parish Mr. Francis did much to encourage the education of the children. To this end Solomon Baker was licenced to teach there on November 19th 1627, and Daniel Swinford was licenced for a similar purpose on April 29th 1630.

Cranbrook about 1800.

Carefully preserved at Ripple are three very important documents which were signed by Rev. Francis and many of his parisioners, and which reveal much of the character of the man.

The first of these is dated 5th May 1641.

A Protestation made by the Honourable House of Commons assembled in Parliament for the upholding and maintaining of the true Protestant Religion according to the doctrine of the Church of England. The words of the Protestation are as follows:

"I A.B. do in the presence of Almighty God promise, vow, and protest to maintain and defend, as far as lawfully I may, with my Life, power, and estate the true reformed Protestant religion expressed in the doctrine of the Church of England, against all popery and Popish innovations within this Realm, contrary to the same doctrine and according to the duty of my Allegiance, his Majesty's Royal person, honour, and estate. As also the power and privilages of parliaments, the lawful rights and liberties of the subject, and every person that maketh this Protestation in whatsoever he shall do in the lawful pursuance of the same. And to my power, and as far as lawfully I may, I will oppose and by all good ways and means' endeavour to bring to condign punishment all such as shall either by force, practise, counsells, plots, conspiracies, or otherwise do any thing to the contrary of anything in this present Protestation contained. And further that I shall in all just and honourable ways endeavour to preserve the union and peace between the three kingdoms of England, Scotland, and Ireland, and neither for hope, fear, nor other respect shall relinquish this promise, vow, and protestation. Whereas some doubts have been raised by several persons out of this house concerning the meaning of these words contained in the Protestation lately made by the members of this House viz, The true Reformed Protestant religion, expressed in the doctrine of the Church of England, against all popery and popish innovations contrary to the same doctrine, This House doth declare that by those words was and is meant only the public doctrine professed in the said Church so far as it is opposite to popery and popish innovations, And that the said words are not to be extended to the maintaining of any form of Worship, Discipline, or Government, nor of any Rites or ceremonies of the said Church of England.

August 15th 1641.

We whose names are underwritten have willingly made the Protestation above written, and do witness it with the subscription of our names

    John Francis, Rector   Thomas Francis
    John Gookin   Edward Francis
    John Stanley   Richard Crayford
    Finch Wilks   Joshua Jacob
    John Taylor   Matthew Raye
    Edward Cocke   Steven Stanley
    Edward Castell   Richard Mackney
    William Burvill   Daniel Longe
    Thomas Mackney   John Philpot
    John Mackney   Steven Harloe
    Edward Staples   Pall Simones
    Edward Browning   William Morris
    John Castell   Nicholas Cornelius   "

It would seem to be worth while to transcribe this somewhat lengthy document in full as it not only reveals the strong Protestant principles which actuated the worthy Rector but also gives us the names of twenty-five of his parishioners at that time. Also it gives us the names of two more of the Francis family, probably his sons.

The second document is entitled, "The Vow and Covenant appoynted by ye Lords and Commons, to be taken throughout the whole kingdome." This is dated June 27th 1643, and was signed by the Rector and thirty parishioners on 28th February 1643–1644.

The third precious document is entitled, "A solemne league and covenant for Reformation and defence of Religion." This was signed by the Rector and twenty-seven parishioners. Collectively these three documents reveal a strong protestant and parliamentary principle in the little village of Ripple during the incumbency of John Francis, which no doubt permeated future generations.

The connection of the Francis family with the town of Cranbrook would appear to have begun with John Francis, the son of John Francis, rector of Ripple.

From the Canterbury Marriage Registers we have the following information "John Francis of Cranbrook, clothier, bachelor, aged about 23 or 24, whose father John Francis, clerk, Rector of Ripple, consents, and Hannah Browne, late of St. James in Dover, now of Ripple, virgin, aged 20, at the government of her uncle Mr. Bartholomew ver Planken of Dover, who also consents. At Ripple, 7th June 1639.

Robert Symons of the Grey Friars Canterbury, gentleman, and John Taylor of St. Peters Canterbury, gentleman, bonds."

The same valuable record also gives the following interesting information regarding the two bondsmen.

"John Taylor of St. Peters Canterbury, gentleman, bachelor, about 28 or 29, with his mother's consent, and Alice Brodnax of Saint Mildreds Canterbury, virgin, about 18, at her own government. At Harbledown or Ripple.

Robert Symons of the Grey Friars Canterbury, gentleman, and Richard Barrow of St. Andrews Canterbury, ironmonger, bonds. 11th February 1640."

John Taylor then went to live at Lyminge where his father was vicar. Robert Symons was the son of Richard Symons of Lyminge and the brother-in-law of John Taylor, as we may learn from the entry of his marriage eleven years before.

"Robert Symons of Lyminge, yeoman, bachelor, about 23, son of Richard Symons, of Lyminge, who consents, and

Frances Taylor of the age of 16, daughter of Jonas Taylor, clerk, parson of Lyminge, who also consents. At Ripple 8th August 1629."

We now complete the full circle of this historical background of the Francis family and Cranbrook when by the death of his wife Hannah, John Francis became a widower and married again, as follows. "John Francis of Cranbrook, clothier, widower, and Alice Taylor, widow of Ripple, widow of John Taylor late of Lyminge, gentleman, deceased. At Cranbrook or Ripple. 24th December 1642."

Throughout the various branches of the Francis Family we find outstanding characteristics of strong religious principles, intellectual ability above their station in life, and exceptional musical ability and talents.

It is however with the generation which sprang from John Francis of Ruckinge near Ashford Kent that we are most concerned as the background of Thomas Clark's famous tune.

John married Sarah Thurston at Ruckinge in December 1768, and had issue in the male line of, (I) William who was born at Ruckinge on 16th December 1773.

In due time William married Hannah Waghorn at Flimwell on the 14th February 1802, and they went to live at Tunbridge Wells. William and Hannah there had issue, first, Jabez. He was born 6th May 1822, and when old enough he was sent to his uncle's school at Cranbrook to be educated. On leaving school Jabez was apprenticed to a printer at Cranbrook, and later entered into partnership with his cousin John in a printing business at Shepherds House Cranbrook. While there he invented and built a special type of printing machine which was so successful that it was produced and exported to different parts of the world.

During this period of his life Jabez frequently visited his sister who lived at Winchelsea in Sussex and, once when staying there he wrote a poem on Winchelsea Castle, which was afterwards published.

The printing business at Shepherds House not proving successful, it was decided to dissolve the partnership, and Jabez thereupon went to live at Rochford in Essex. In his new home he soon established himself as a reputable printer, and with the help of only the local blacksmith he built several excellent two manual organs. He proved himself a

The old studios and former home of Thomas Webster, R.A.

musician of outstanding ability, and composed a number of very singable hymn tunes.

The other child of William and Hannah Francis was named Elizabeth, and she was born at Tunbridge Wells, and later went to live at Winchelsea where she married the Rev. Oliver, who was later Congregational minister at Great Watering, Essex.

John and Sarah Francis had a daughter Sarah who at the age of 19 married John Lester of Warehorn, at Ruckinge, 29th October 1791.

The second son of John and Sarah Francis was named John, and he was born at Ruckinge in 1776. He early revealed a very studious disposition and an outstanding talent for singing, which fitted him well for his chosen profession of schoolmaster. In due time he went to live at Cranbrook where he married Miss Blundell, a schoolmistress, who was the daughter of Mr. Stephen Blundell, a veterinary surgeon of High Street, Cranbrook.

We next hear of John Francis as the proprietor of a very successful private school known as Shepherds House Boarding School, High Street, Cranbrook. The impressive size and obvious importance of Shepherds House may be taken as some indication of the position in life attained by John Francis. The house had been built in 1554 by Thomas Sheafe, a leading clothier of that period, on the site of an earlier house. In this connection it is of interest to note that a Thomas Sheafe and a Richard Sheafe signed one of the famous documents at Ripple on 28th February 1643. From the Cranbrook Church warden's accounts we learn that Richard Sheafe was fined ten shillings in 1665 for being taken at a Conventicle and was convicted.

After the decline of the cloth trade Shepherds House was purchased by a member of the Hope family who were doctors in the town.

In the time of John Francis, about 1830, the old house was described as being typically Elizabethan in character, having many rooms, and twenty-one windows in front. An outstanding feature of the large entrance hall was a massive broad oak staircase leading up to a great timber gallery along one side. The wall on the opposite side of the hall was covered with tapestry depicting life-sized figures. In this large old house John Francis provided accommodation for forty boys.

According to family tradition it was in Shepherds House that John Francis junior was born as the result of an illicit love affair between John Francis senior and the wife of Mr. Lewis Green, a nearby grocer. Naturally young John received a good education, and when old enough entered into partnership with his father under the title of John Francis and Son, Academy, High Street, Cranbrook.

Unfortunately John junior was not of the same studious nature as was his father and he showed a strong preference to work with his hands. Consequently when the time came for his father to retire, the school was closed down, and John entered into partnership with his cousin Jabez in the printing business.

The Marriage Register would seem to suggest that John then formed an alliance with his mother's family, as follows.

"John Francis of Cranbrook, bachelor, 23, and Elizabeth Green of Maidstone, spinster, 25, at Maidstone, 3rd January 1837."

The printing business prospered for a time, and then John lost interest in it, and proved a very unsatisfactory partner for his more industrious and intelligent cousin. Jabez therefore, as has already been described, dissolved the partnership, and went to Rochford in Essex where he established a similar business.

After the printing business had been closed down the two wings of the grand old Shepherds House were demolished, and the central portion was altered to its present appearance. At the time of the alterations some of the old oak panelling was bought by the then master of Cranbrook School and used to panel one of the rooms in the school house, where it may still be seen.

On his retirement from Shepherds House, John Francis senior had built for himself a house on St. Davids Hill, Cranbrook, which he named Albion Cottage. An interesting feature of this house was the flat roof, on which the owner often relaxed while he smoked his pipe and enjoyed the magnificent view. Under the overhanging eaves he stretched taught wires which, when the wind blew on them, gave out musical tones and acted like an aolean harp. Amusement was caused when passers-by stopped and listened to the tones, thinking that the sound came from the organ in the distant church.

During recent years, Albion Cottage, having been unoccupied for some time, had become derelict and was consequently condemned by the local Council. Fortunately however someone saw possibilities in the old building and restored it to its present habitable condition by giving it a new roof.

The third son of John and Sarah Francis was born at Ruckinge in 1783, and was named James. Having received a basic education he was then apprenticed to Mr. William Clark of St. Georges Street, Canterbury, as a cordwainer. Although he was some eight years younger than Thomas Clark there was thus formed the firm link of a life-long friendship. Living, as he did in the Clark home, and moving in musical circles with Thomas, young James Francis had every encouragement to develop his natural musical talent to the full.

Wherever Thomas Clark went to organise or perform at church anniversaries, or to ring church bells, young James Francis was his constant companion. Under this influence, not only did he compose much music, and play with some accomplishment several instruments, but possessing a fine voice he became a singer of some renown. He was often in demand, sometimes travelling to distant parts of the country to sing solos. In due time he married and went to live at Faversham, where he was in business as a boot-maker. He raised a large family there, among whom were three very talented and musical sons, namely, Frederick, Walter, and Edward.

An interesting story is told of Frederick who, when he was a boy, was one day sent to deliver some boots which his father had made for Lord Sondes of Lees Court, Faversham. His Lordship saw the young man and stopping him asked, what is your name my boy? Francis, my Lord, replied the boy. Are you the son of Francis who sings? Yes my Lord. Can you sing too? Yes my Lord. Let me hear you then. Frederick thereupon sang a song of four verses with a refrain entitled 'Money is your friend'. When the lad had finished Lord Sondes expressed his pleasure, and turning to his servant said, "Give the boy a sovereign".

Frederick fulfilled his early promise and grew up to be a Professor of Music and establish a music shop in the High Street, Cranbrook. His son, Thomas Ditch Francis, of Waterloo Place, Cranbrook, was also described as a Professor of Music, and was for many years organist of St. Dunstans church there. He died about the year 1910.

Both of Frederick's two brothers were friends of Thomas Clark, and he was often a visitor in their homes. Walter Francis settled at Green Street, now known as Teynham, near Faversham, and Edward Francis went to live at Warehorn where his aunt lived. Like the other members of the family they were both accomplished musicians and singers.

Thomas Clark loved to visit his friends at Cranbrook and to ring the bells of the church there. There is a strong tradition which has been handed down through the successive generations of the Francis family that Thomas Clark always came to Cranbrook with a bundle of new tunes, which the boys of Shepherds House School copied out and then sang for him to enable him to perfect them before they went to the printer. It was for the forty strong choir of that school that he composed the tune Cranbrook, which was destined to become his most famous tune. When in 1805 Clark was able to publish his "First Set of Psalm and Hymn Tunes", his tune Cranbrook appeared in print for the first time at No. 20.

The tune achieved immediate popularity and captured the favour of churches of all denominations. It was printed again and again, set to different words and printed in many hymn books. At first it was sung most frequently either to hymn No. 3 in Dr. Rippon's Collection, or to Dr. Watt's version of Psalm 45, "My Saviour and my King". Nevertheless time and custom has failed to create a better union than that with Dr. Philip Dodderidge's well-known hymn, "Grace 'tis a charming sound". Dr. Dodderidge never heard his famous hymn sung to this tune as he died on the 26th October 1751, leaving his hymn in manuscript, and it was not published until 1755, by his friend Job Orton.

Thomas Clark himself favoured the singing of his tune to Dodderidge's hymn. One who well remembered the old composer training the Anniversary Choir at the Baptist Chapel at Eythorne has described how he urged the choir to give every ounce of their strength at the words, "And all the earth shall hear".

Thomas Webster R.A., was a famous artist who lived for most of his life at Cranbrook, and died there on the 23rd September 1886. He used his art to depict the quaint church choir there in 1847, and it is a picture which has been reproduced many times as a good example of a typical church choir of those days. Similar choirs have also been immortalised by Thomas Hardy in his well-known books, "Under the Greenwood Tree", and "The Return of the Native".

It has always been affirmed in the Francis family that in Thomas Webster's famous picture the conductor of the choir is none other than John Francis senior, and that Thomas Clark is depicted playing the clarionet which was bought by the church wardens in 1802.

In his "Life of Charles H. Spurgeon", the Rev. R. Shindler affirms that the favourite hymn of the great preacher was, "Grace 'tis a charming sound", which he always sang to the tune Cranbrook.

A selection of Thomas Clark's most well known tunes

Burnham. 4-6's & 2-8's.

T. CLARK.

1. Rejoice, the Lord is King! Your Lord and King adore; Mortals, give thanks, and sing, And triumph evermore: Lift up your heart, lift up your voice, Lift up your heart, lift up your voice, Rejoice! Rejoice! again I say, rejoice!

2 Jesus the Saviour reigns,
　The God of truth and love;
When He had purged our stains,
　He took His seat above:
Lift up your heart, lift up your voice,
Rejoice, again I say, rejoice!

3 His kingdom cannot fail;
　He rules o'er earth and heaven;
The keys of death and hell
　Are to our Jesus given:
Lift up your heart, lift up your voice,
Rejoice, again I say, rejoice!

4 He sits at God's right hand
　Till all His foes submit,
And bow to His command,
　And fall beneath His feet:
Lift up your heart, lift up your voice,
Rejoice, again I say, rejoice!

5 He all His foes shall quell,
　Shall all our sins destroy,
And every bosom swell
　With pure seraphic joy:
Lift up your heart, lift up your voice,
Rejoice, again I say, rejoice!

6 Rejoice in glorious hope,
　Jesus the Judge shall come,
And take His servants up
　To their eternal home:
We soon shall hear the archangel's voice,
The trump of God shall sound, Rejoice!

Calcutta. 8.7.8.7.4.7.

T. CLARK.

2 Every eye shall now behold Him
  Robed in dreadful majesty ;
Those who set at nought and sold Him,
  Pierced and nailed Him to the tree,
    Deeply wailing,
  Shall the true Messiah see.

3 The dear tokens of His passion
  Still His dazzling body bears ;
Cause of endless exultation
  To His ransomed worshippers ;
    With what rapture
  Gaze we on those glorious scars !

4 Yea, Amen ! let all adore Thee,
    High on Thy eternal throne ;
  Saviour, take the power and glory,
    Claim the kingdom for Thine own ;
      Jah, Jehovah,
    Everlasting God, come down !

Cornhill. S.M.

DR. WATTS.
T. CLARK.

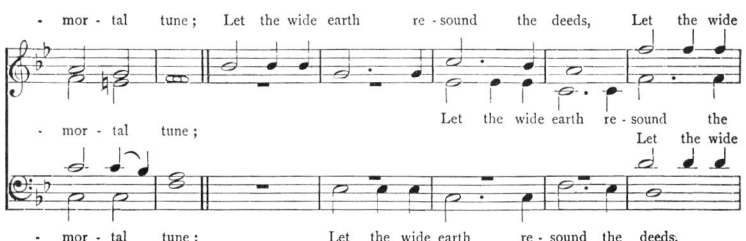
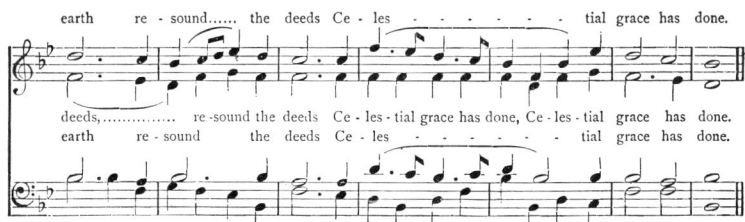

2.
Sing how eternal love
Its Chief Beloved chose,
And bid Him raise our wretched race
From their abyss of woes.

3.
His hand no thunder bears,
No terror clothes His brow ;
No bolts to drive our guilty souls
To fiercer flames below,

4.
'Twas mercy filled the throne,
And wrath stood silent by,
When Christ was sent with pardons down
To rebels doomed to die.

5.
Now, sinners, dry your tears,
Let hopeless sorrows cease ;
Bow to the sceptre of His love,
And take the offered peace.

6.
Lord, we obey Thy call,
We lay an humble claim
To the salvation Thou hast brought,
And love and praise Thy name.

2. Grace first contrived a way
   To save rebellious man ;
   And all the steps *that* grace display
   Which drew the wondrous plan.

3. Grace taught my wandering feet
   To tread the heavenly road ;
   And new supplies each hour I meet
   While pressing on to God.

4. Grace all the work shall crown
   Through everlasting days ,
   It lays in heaven the topmost stone,
   And well deserves the praise.

CREDITON.   C.M.   T. Clark, 1775-1859.

1 I KNOW that my Redeemer lives,
   And ever prays for me;
   A token of His love He gives,
   A pledge of liberty.

2 I find Him lifting up my head,
   He brings salvation near,
   His presence makes me free indeed,
   And He will soon appear.

3 He wills that I should holy be;
   What can withstand His will?
   The counsel of His grace in me
   He surely shall fulfil.

4 Jesus, I hang upon Thy word;
   I steadfastly believe
   Thou wilt return and claim me, Lord,
   And to Thyself receive.

5 When God is mine, and I am His,
   Of paradise possessed,
   I taste unutterable bliss
   And everlasting rest.

Charles Wesley, **1707-88.**

2.
Well pleased the husbandmen behold
  The waving yellow crop;
With joy they bear the sheaves away,
  And sow again in hope.

3.
Thus teach me, gracious God, to sow
  The seeds of righteousness
Smile on my soul, and with Thy beams
  The ripening harvest bless.

Rose Lane

C.M.
T. CLARK.

1 FATHER of Jesus Christ, my Lord,
  My Saviour, and my Head,
  I trust in Thee, whose powerful word
  Hath raised Him from the dead.

2 Faith, mighty faith, the promise sees,
  And looks to that alone;
  Laughs at impossibilities,
  And cries, It shall be done!

3 To Thee the glory of Thy power
  And faithfulness I give;
  I shall in Christ, in that glad hour,
  And Christ in me shall live.

4 Obedient faith, that waits on Thee,
  Thou never wilt reprove:
  But Thou wilt form Thy Son in me,
  And perfect me in love.

SYRIA. 7 7.7 7. D. *Union Tune Book*, 1842.

1. Holy Lamb, who Thee confess,
Followers of Thy holiness,
Thee they ever keep in view,
Ever ask : What shall we do ?
Governed by Thy only will,
All Thy words we would fulfil,
Would in all Thy footsteps go,
Walk as Jesus walked below.

2. While Thou didst on earth appear,
Servant to Thy servants here,
Mindful of Thy place above,
All Thy life was prayer and love.
Such our whole employment be,
Works of faith and charity ;
Works of love on man bestowed,
Secret intercourse with God.

3. Early in the temple met,
Let us still our Saviour greet ;
Nightly to the mount repair,
Join our praying Pattern there.
There by wrestling faith obtain
Power to work for God again,
Power His image to retrieve,
Power, like Thee, our Lord, to live.

4. Vessels, instruments of grace,
Pass we thus our happy days
'Twixt the mount and multitude,
Doing or receiving good,;
Glad to pray and labour on,
Till our earthly course is run,
Till we, on the sacred tree,
Bow the head and die like Thee.

Charles Wesley, 1707-88.

Twyford (or Jethro). C.M.

T. CLARK.

2 In darkest shades, if Thou appear,
  My dawning is begun;
 Thou art my soul's bright morning star,
  And Thou my rising sun.

3 The opening heavens around me shine
  With beams of sacred bliss,
 If Jesus shows His mercy mine,
  And whispers I am His.

4 My soul would leave this heavy clay
  At that transporting word;
 Run up with joy the shining way,
  To see and praise my Lord.

WARSAW. 6.6.6.6.8 8. T. Clark, 1775-1859.

1 Come, all whoe'er have set
    Your faces Zion-ward,
  In Jesus let us meet,
    And praise our common Lord;
  In Jesus let us still go on,
  Till all appear before His throne.

2 Nearer, and nearer still,
    We to our country come,
  To that celestial hill,
    The weary pilgrim's home:
  The new Jerusalem above,
  The seat of everlasting love.

3 The peace and joy of faith
    Each moment may we feel;
  Redeemed from sin and wrath,
    From earth, and death, and hell,
  We to our Father's house repair,
  To meet our elder Brother there.

4 Our Brother, Saviour, Head,
    Our all in all, is He;
  And in His steps who tread
    We soon His face shall see;
  Shall see Him with our glorious friends,
  And then in heaven our journey ends.
            Charles Wesley, 1707-88.

For Little Children

ATHENS. Irregular.

1 I THINK, when I read that sweet story of old,
   When Jesus was here among men,
How He called little children as lambs to His fold,
   I should like to have been with them then;
I wish that His hands had been placed on my head,
   That His arms had been thrown around me,
And that I might have seen His kind look when He said;
   Let the little ones come unto Me!

2 Yet still to His footstool in prayer I may go,
   And ask for a share in His love;
And if I now earnestly seek Him below,
   I shall see Him and hear Him above,
In that beautiful place He is gone to prepare
   For all who are washed and forgiven;
And many dear children are gathering there,
   For of such is the kingdom of heaven.